P9-EET-168

THAT WE MAY PERFECTLY LOVE THEE

THAT WE MAY PERFECTLY LOVE THEE

Preparing Our Hearts for Holy Communion

Robert Benson

UPPER
ROOM BOOKS®
NASHVILLE

THAT WE MAY PERFECTLY LOVE THEE: Preparing Our Hearts for Holy Communion
Copyright © 2011 Robert Benson
All rights reserved.

Originally published by Paraclete Press as *That We May Perfectly Love Thee: Preparing Our Hearts for the Eucharist* (ISBN 1-55725-300-5). Copyright © 2002 by Robert Benson.

The epigraphs preceding each chapter are taken from The Book of Common Prayer, published by the Church Hymnal Corporation, New York, in 1979. Some of these texts have been adapted by the author and are indicated by the symbol †.

No part of this book may be reproduced in any manner whatsoever without written permission of the publisher except in brief quotations embodied in critical articles or reviews. For information, write Upper Room Books, 1908 Grand Avenue, Nashville, TN 37212.

The Upper Room Web site: www.upperroom.org.

UPPER ROOM®, UPPER ROOM BOOKS®, and design logos are trademarks owned by The Upper Room®, a ministry of GBOD®, Nashville, Tennessee. All rights reserved.

Unless otherwise indicated, scripture quotations are taken from the New Revised Standard Version Bible, copyright © 1989, Division of Christian Education of the National Council of Churches of Christ in the United States of America. Used by permission. All rights reserved.

Cover and Interior Design: Christa Schoenbrodt, Studio Haus

Library of Congress Cataloging-in-Publication Data
Benson, R. (Robert), 1952–
  That we may perfectly love Thee: preparing our hearts for Holy Communion /
by Robert Benson.
     p. cm.
  Includes bibliographical references (p.   ).
  ISBN 978-0-8358-1093-7
  1. Lord's Supper—Episcopal Church. I. Title.
  BX5949.C5B46 2012
  264'.36—dc23
                                          2011036059

Printed in the United States of America.

This book is for Anne and Kenneth and Geoffrey and Michael,
and all who seek to perfect the praises of God's people.
And it is for all who join with them.
And it is, as always,
for the Friends of Silence & of the Poor

CONTENTS

CHAPTER 1

The Voluntary

I was glad when they said unto me:
Let us go to the house of the Lord.[†]

A PRAYER FOR THE MORNING

Almighty and ever living God: You have sustained us
through the darkness, and you have blessed us with life in
this new day. In the shadow of your wings, we sing for joy,
and bless your holy Name. Amen.

On the Sundays that I can, the Sundays when I do not have to travel, the Sundays on which I am in the city where I live and have slept under my own roof and can go to worship with the people that I love and alongside the people who call me by my name when I am among them, I like to rise early, before the sun if I can. It is a way of keeping the sabbath for me.

Of all of the Sundays that I have lived, these are the ones that I have come to treasure the most. They are the ones that are the most ordinary to me and yet the most sacred at the same time.

— • —

There is the blue-black of the sky just before the sun begins its daily journey to the other side of the horizon. There are the long red streaks in the sky that remind you that the dark night will indeed end before too long. And then the birds begin, chirping and chattering and whistling. These days, as I write this, it is late summer—almost autumn—and the birds are beginning to congregate regularly around the feeders in our yard, especially the one that I hung from the roof of the front porch. I put it there so that I can see the chickadees through the window across the room from where I sit cross-legged in the corner of a little couch, nursing a cup of coffee and scribbling prayer of a sort in a sketch book, and waiting to see what manner of day this will be that the Lord has made.

It is Sunday, and the one word that I will do my best not to say today is "hurry."

— • —

"What the church does first and foremost," writes Jeffrey Lee in *Opening the Prayer Book*, "is worship the living God." His statement is not poetic, but it is not to be taken lightly. What we do with this day, in our homes and in our hearts, in our churches and in our cathedrals, in our auditoriums and in our sanctuaries is the one thing that matters the most. This day that we call Sunday, the sabbath, is the day when we are called to worship the Living God with the utmost faithfulness and reverence and devotion. And this service, the service of Word and Table—the Eucharist, the Holy Communion, the Blessed Sacrament, the Lord's Supper, whatever name is used for it in the community with which we gather—this is the act of worship that we are called to offer up.

This is a critical part of our life together, I think to myself sometimes. It seems critically important that we approach this act of praise and thanksgiving with some measure of reverence and attention to its art and its history and its tradition.

And it is hard for me to do so sometimes, because I live in a busy, complex society, where I spend much of my time trying to do so many things at once. It is often difficult for me to respond to a call to observe the sabbath with anything resembling the sort of single-mindedness that is required.

It is hard too because so many of us worship now in places that we did not grow up in. And the practices of the communities where we find ourselves now may still be somewhat unfamiliar to us, and we may not understand them, neither in their individual parts nor as a whole.

On the other hand, some of us worship in places where what happens at worship is so familiar to us that we have come to take what happens for granted somehow, and go through it all with little wonder or awe at what is being said and done.

Many of us, too, have spent some of our journey in places where the worship services are so weighted toward one part of worship or the other—the praise and singing part, or the sermon part, or the Communion part—that we may have little sense of them as a whole. It is hard to prepare one's heart for the liturgy of Word and Table if one does not know even a little about the connections between the two.

There is another thing that happens sometimes as well. Sometimes our age of consumerism gets the better of us even in our pews, and we approach our worship with an eye toward getting something out of it for ourselves rather than with an eye toward what we are to give to it. Our participation in the mystery of the Eucharist is colored by our desire to be sure that there is something in it for us rather than for the One Whom we worship. The truth is that what we do this day in the name of worship is not even for us; it is for the Living God.

— • —

For centuries now, theologians have referred to the Eucharist most commonly as a mystery. This whole business of gathering up for the service of Word and Table is so rich and complex and layered with meaning that I can hardly get my heart and mind around it sometimes. It is still mysterious, all these centuries later, to me and to everyone else who is beginning this Lord's day, however their day of worship and rest begins. I wish that I knew more about this mystery than I know now.

Like most everyone else who will enter into the courts of praise this day, whatever it is that I know about any of these things I have learned the same way that the others have—from sitting in the pew, and from reading books that one wise friend or another has recommended, and from asking questions of various and sundry patient souls who have traveled this way before. Our teachers, as it were, have been many and varied—priests and monks and poets and saints and artists and fellow strugglers and stumblers. Many of them we have never met, save in the pages of their books, and many of them died centuries before we even came along with the questions that we have about the things that all of us who sit in the pews and try to worship have always asked.

Sometimes, on these early sabbath mornings, their faces and voices will come to mind for me, and I will remember what they taught me about preparing my heart and mind and soul so that I may worship in spirit and in truth on this day. Sometimes I will pull out an old book, one that has meant some particular thing to me along my journey, and I will look again at the lines that I have marked, and I remember what they have meant to me over the years.

— • —

I think of my father on these early sabbath mornings, as I sit waiting for the sun to rise and the house to wake up and the day to begin. He was responsible for a lot of this, in a way. He was the one who taught me to get up early and to go to church on Sundays. I remember being young and being upstairs sleeping as late as possible on a Sunday morning—like the two who are upstairs from me just now. I can remember the sound of hymns playing on the stereo downstairs as the house began to stir. I was happy enough then to be startled awake by my parents, then crash through the shower and my closet in a hurry. I would try my best to walk the fine line between not having to be awake any sooner than I absolutely had to and not being the one who made us all late to church.

Now that I am older and I am the one whose role it is to wake the house for the observance of the sabbath, I try to move slowly and quietly and gently, even reverently, I hope, into such days. What I am looking for, it seems to me, is some clarity of purpose, some quickening of the spirit, some focus to my thoughts so that I may respond to the call to worship. For if we cannot love our God with all our heart and with all our soul and with all our mind and with all our strength on this day of all days, how will we do so come the complexities of our lives next Thursday afternoon, when the children are tired and the work does not go well and the news is dark and ominous?

"Lift up your hearts," they will say in a little while when we gather. And I want very badly to be able to do so indeed. I am hopeful of at least that.

I have learned that if I will pay attention from the very beginning of the day, there will be reminder after reminder that this day—as all days do, of course, even the days each week that are given over to work and to school and to travel and all the rest—that this day of all days each week belongs to the One Who made us, the One Who sustains us, the One Who has chosen, inexplicably it seems to me sometimes, to bless us with life in this new day.

— • —

The coffee is finished now, the birds have gone off to other yards in the neighborhood on their daily rounds, and my knees have begun to ache from sitting here so long. It is time to wake the ones to whom I have been given and who have been given to me. It is time for us to go unto the house of the Lord, to join with all those who would enter his courts with praise. It is time to make our entrance, together, with a hymn of worship and honor and adoration, time to hear the Word proclaimed, time to offer our prayers and offerings and thanksgivings. And it is time to come to the Table of the Lord, where the Word Made Flesh will be broken and shared.

Let us rejoice and be glad together.

CHAPTER 2

The Entrance

FROM THE PSALTER

*Lord, we love the house in which you dwell,
and the place where your glory abides.*†

A PRAYER BEFORE WORSHIP — FROM THE HOLY EUCHARIST

*Glory to God in the highest;
and peace to his people on earth.*

These days when I go to worship on Sunday, I go to an Episcopal cathedral in the heart of the city where I live. It is a grand old place—more than one hundred years old, in fact—a great sandstone building full of dark and shadow and art and tradition and history.

It is always hushed and quiet when we arrive, and it is customary in such places to enter and depart in silence, allowing for those who are there with you to be at prayer both before and after the service. That is not the custom at all places, I know; but it is a good practice it seems to me.

As we make our way down the aisle, our footsteps echo on the flagstone floors. On either side of us, there are always people at the kneeling benches in each pew, heads bowed in prayer. There are always people sitting quietly as well, hands folded and eyes closed, listening to an inner Voice, or at least seeking it. For some gathered here, these few moments before the service begins in this great hall are the only truly quiet moments in an entire week of their busy lives. To interrupt such moments seems an unseemly thing to do as we begin our communal praise of the Almighty.

We generally head in the direction of the first pew, on the "epistle side" as they say. We like to be near the front; it is a way to cut down on distractions. And we like to be able to see everything that goes on and to hear the singing of both the choir and the congregation. We bow to the altar before us, reverence it each in our own way as well, slip in to our places, and begin to pray.

After a few moments, we begin to flip our way through the worship folder for the day, noting the season and the day and the speaker and the hymns. We arrange the little bookmarks in our prayer books and hymnals. I did not grow up in the Episcopal Church, and I have learned the hard way that even if my heart is not ready for worship, then my bookmarks better be or the service will go off and leave me.

Sometimes one of our friends who sits in the same section of the church will pass by and tap us on the shoulder in greeting, and we will exchange smiles and nods. Sometimes we simply wait in stillness and silence.

As I wait, it occurs to me sometimes that I am as at home here as I am anywhere on earth. I wonder if God will feel the same before this service has ended.

— • —

There are some of us who still go to church on Sunday in the same church in which we grew up. But there are not so many who can say that anymore. Like a lot of people, I have moved around some in my life, both geographically and spiritually.

The first place that I remember going to church was in Winter Park, Florida. I attended Lawndale Nazarene Church because my father was the pastor. It did not take very long for us to travel to church on Sunday mornings: A door from our kitchen led directly into the sanctuary. We lived in four rooms in the back of the church. A Sunday school class met in my bedroom and another in our kitchen. My mother played the piano, and my father preached and led the singing, and my brother and I sat on the front row in the care of some lady in the church whose job it was to make sure that we behaved.

When I was nine, we moved to Nashville, Tennessee, the city that had always been home to my parents and that has been home to me pretty much ever since. When we moved, our family began to attend the First Church of the Nazarene. It was the church that my great-grandfather helped to build and the place where my grandfather was the song leader and the place where my parents got married. It was there, among those good people, who began to teach me the Story and to show me its ways, that I learned that when it was Sunday, it was time to go to church. That was the place where I first began to learn about the "regular attendance to the private and public worship of God," as they say in the community to which I now belong.

The sanctuary itself was a large room with wooden pews, enough for nine hundred people or so, if you counted the ones in the balcony that wrapped around both sides and up into the back wall. The pulpit, as is generally the case in Nazarene settings, was in the center of the chancel. Up behind it rose the eight or ten rows of pews that formed the choir loft, and behind that rose the short glass wall that marked the edge of the baptismal pool. A wooden altar, wrapped in a sort of circle around the chancel, came equipped with kneeling pads and a row of little round circles where you placed the Communion cups when you had finished—though we generally took Communion in the pews, as I recall. I remember the altar because I was there pretty often. I was "praying through," as they called it, and did so a fair amount when I was young, surrounded by most of the people who loved me first and best in my life.

As it turned out, I could not stay among these good people for my whole journey home to God. I was led to other places and to other houses of worship. But that place still holds a place in my heart.

Years later, after some traveling—both geographical and spiritual—I was welcomed into the community that gathered up on the other side of the river at West End United Methodist Church. There are only about thirty city blocks and a river in between them. If I stand in the tower of the cathedral that I now attend, I am standing in a direct line about halfway between the two. I can look east and see the steeple of the church where I grew up just across the river, and I can look west about the same distance and see the tower at West End where I was welcomed back into the household of faith with open arms. The three houses of the Lord to which I owe almost everything are all in plain sight of one another.

— • —

It is hard, perhaps impossible in a way, to separate a sense of place from a sense of worship. Perhaps it is not even wise to attempt to do so.

"We can worship God anywhere," some say, "so why does where we worship matter?" But the truth is that place has long mattered to those have gone before us and worshiped the One Who made us.

The Story told in the scriptures tells the stories of those who gathered up stones and built altars in the wilderness of the ancient Near East to remember and to proclaim and to honor the memory and the presence of Yahweh. "Here I raise my Ebenezer," said Samuel, the altar builder. And others followed in his footsteps and are following still, building altars and temples, chapels and cathedrals; and we would be wise to remember this as we take our places in the places where we go to worship.

The signs that we see along the road from time to time, the ones that say "Future Home of the Such-and-Such Church," may bear little resemblance to Samuel's pile of stones, but their meaning is the same. It is a sign that marks some community's belief that they too have been called to raise up something to the glory of God. At some point, the place that you enter on this day was little more than a promise that a group of people made to God and to one another. It was then and is now a sign that some of God's faithful had gathered themselves up to pool their resources and their time and their talent and their hope to raise up this place through whose doors you walk this very morning. It is holy ground that you walk upon; it is the house of God.

— • —

All places of worship are not the same. They vary according to the community that has raised them up, reflecting different resources and traditions, particular sensibilities and missions.

Some of them are great and grand places. They are full of art and of architecture and of wonder. We cannot describe them without using words like nave and chancel and high altar and transepts and such. They are full of marble and stone and wood that has been ornately carved. They carry in their very walls a reminder of the great temples of worship that began to be constructed in the time of Constantine, in the days of the church's sudden and astonishing move from intimate and often secret gatherings in catacombs and houses to grand and public places. They hearken back to the medieval days of Europe, to the days of the great cathedrals, the days when great artisans and artists, both celebrated ones and unknown ones, did their work at the behest of the church and for the glory of God.

In such places, every detail, every texture and color and fixture has some rich meaning that, despite its having its roots in our Christian tradition, is all too often unknown to us moderns. To step into any of them is to glimpse the aesthetic and worship sensibilities of those who have gone before us, those who are the mothers and fathers of our faith. There is the cruciform floor plan in which the nave and the transepts and the chancel form the shape of the Latin cross. There is the breathtaking tracery—delicate carvings in wood and stone—that surrounds the windows and the altar and the altar screens and the like.

Such places inspire in us a kind of awe and reverence and can leave us breathless, especially when we are unfamiliar with them—and rightly so. More than once I have seen people who have been brought to tears by their first visit to such a place. "That someone made this for the glory of God," I heard someone whisper through her tears one day, standing in the back of the Cathedral of St. John the Divine in New York City.

Some of us worship in places that remind us of the spread of our faith across our land in the early years of our nation's history—the houses of worship that our ancestors attended. Such places remind us of the stories and the spirits of the people who built our nation, and they give us a sense of their need to honor the One who made it possible for us to become a nation. They are brick and stone and austere and rugged, in a way that speaks to us still of the birth of our cities and our towns and, indeed, our culture as a whole. Some of them are wooden churches, found in the countryside, buildings raised up by a group of people who had likely gathered together the spring before to raise a barn or a schoolhouse as well. Well-worn board floors and hard-backed pews and simple furnishings speak to us of the hearts and the lives and the times of those who raised their Ebenezer there.

Some of the places where we worship are more modern in spirit, if you will, in the ways that they are constructed. Rather than cathedrals, they are auditoriums built to accommodate large crowds. As such they remind us of the way that the Roman basilicas were built in the fifth and sixth centuries of the church. They have big, wide chancels with pulpits in the center. Their very design often reflects a shift from the formal and liturgical to the more free-form and sermon-driven worship of the evangelical church. They have sound systems that actually work and a kind of big and open American feel that is inviting and warm and familiar. They are full of light rather than shadow, full of openness rather than mystery. They are less about art and more about function, and as such they reflect yet another sense of what it means to be the people of God.

Some of us worship in other places, of course—gymnasiums and office parks and school buildings. And in houses and little chapels of every description. Place does not matter in the sense that it matters how grand the edifice or how traditional the architecture. What matters is that it is a home for God.

What matters is that we remember that this place— whatever it is and wherever it is and whatever it is that it looks

like, this place is the house of the Lord. And that what we have
come here to do on this day is to worship the One Who has
made us and not we ourselves. And that everything that happens
here is not for us at all; it is for God.

— • —

There is no right place, of course. None of them is necessarily, by
virtue of its architecture or its furnishings or its layout, more holy
than another. The building itself does not make our worship
holy; it is the other way around. It is our worship that makes the
building holy.

In the place where I worship these days, a priest will come
down into the center of the room to read the Gospel lesson for
the day, signifying the coming of God among us. Where I grew
up, the Gospel was read from the pulpit. In one place baptisms
take place in the front of the room so that all can see and so
that those being baptized can make a sort of statement to their
brothers and their sisters as they go forward to publicly be joined
with them. In the other, the font is in the back of the room, and
those who are to be baptized go out among us from the front
of the room and return more one of us than they were before.
Where I worship now, we are invited to the Table itself to receive
the bread and the cup. Where I grew up, the Body that was

broken and the Blood that was shed were passed through the aisles, and we served one another.

When I was younger, I used to worry a great deal about whether things were done the right way. Over time I have come to see the beauty in the tradition of coming forward to the altar to kneel and be served. But I have also come to see the sense of community that is evidenced by sitting in a small circle and serving and being served the Holy Mysteries by your brother or your sister. I have come to treasure the sense of being connected to the great traditions of the church that is given witness in some places by the insistence on only priests or deacons being allowed to serve. I have come to have a sense of the power of sharing a common cup, as well as the power of holding one cup that is only for me, reminding me that the blood that was shed was not only for everyone in general, it was for me in the specific as well.

I am, like most everyone, comfortable with the things that are familiar to me, especially when it comes to the things that are so important to me. But I am finally far enough along on my journey to have come to see that the variations on the liturgical dance, as well as the variations in architecture and symbolism and form, are not at odds with one another; they are simply different ways of saying the same things. I no longer worship regularly in the same sort of room that I did when I began my journey. Nor do I sing the same sort of hymns or hear the same sort of sermons or come to the same sort of Table to be served in the same sort of way. I was led to where I am by God, to be in this place, among these people, to practice the act of worship and thanksgiving with them in the way that they practice it. I am finally far enough along in my journey to be grateful to be in a room with the Table on this day and to be present among those who seek a glimpse of the truths that are hidden in plain sight in its mysteries.

— • —

I heard a priest say, as he began his sermon one Christmas Eve after the Nativity story was read, that the Story had rolled its way through the darkness across the whole wide world, from church to church, pulpit to pulpit, community to community, until now it was our turn to tell it.

Such a thing happens each and every Sunday morning as well. The praise and worship of the One Who made us has rolled its way through the darkness, following the rising sun, until it has found its way here to where we wait for the bells to ring and the procession to begin and the organ to play. And it carries with it all our collective praise and worship through the years, and it carries with it all our collective responsibility to ascribe unto the Lord the honor due God's Name. It binds us together as the people of God, as the people for whom the Christ came and for whom the Body was broken and shared for all time.

Such a thing calls indeed for silence and awe and reverence, regardless of what sort of place we are sitting in as we wait for our worship to begin, regardless of what our community's Ebenezer looks like, as we wait to begin the rituals and customs and practices that will lead us to the Table of the Lord.

CHAPTER 3

The Work of God

Accept, O God, the willing tribute of my lips,
and teach me your ways.†

A PRAYER BEFORE WORSHIP — FROM THE HOLY EUCHARIST

The Lord be with you.
And also with you.
Let us pray.

We sit in our place and watch as the acolytes and the choir and the deacons and the priests gather up in the doorway to the hall just to our right, listening as the organist finishes the voluntary. Soon the entrance hymn will begin, and the procession will start.

The procession will go up the aisle past us on the right, and we will join the others in our pew in bowing before the cross as it passes and is carried to the back of the nave. Then it will come

through the center, this great procession, and we will turn slightly
so that we can see them as they come through the aisle to pass
on our left this time, all of our voices raised in song. The acolytes,
the sopranos, the altos, the tenors, the basses, the servers, and the
priests will go past. They will pause and bow before the altar as
they take their places. This is what I was anticipating early this
morning as I sat in my front room. *This is what we have come for.
This is why we are here*, I think to myself.

I have lived some twenty-five hundred Sundays or so. On
a fair number of them, I have spent a fair portion of the day at
church. I have long ago turned in my perfect attendance pin, but
I have been gathered up with the faithful more often than not.
And gladly so. I am not particularly anxious for the day that the
saints go marching in, but I do like our dress rehearsals, and
especially the procession.

Some days and in some places, only the priests and the
ministers process; sometimes it is a small army, it seems. Always
it calls to mind for me the story of the entry of Jesus into
Jerusalem with songs and shouts. Other times it makes me think
of a time when churches stood on a hill in the towns and the
villages of Christendom, and there was indeed a procession of
all up the hill to worship. Sometimes I imagine that I can see the
psalmist himself, leading the parade to the temple and leading
the multitudes in the festal shout.

Some days when the procession goes past, I am thinking about Bardstown, Kentucky. It is a place I have never lived in but think of as a kind of birthplace.

— • —

For reasons that I can no longer remember, I found myself on a Sunday morning in Bardstown, and I walked the two or three blocks or so from the inn where I was staying to a small brick church just off the square. It was an Episcopal church, whose name I cannot recall.

By that time in my life, I had been attending the Episcopal Church for some time, and I had even begun to go to the classes that they offer to those who want to become card-carrying members. The liturgy and the worship of the church were what had drawn me, and I was learning to love them and to participate in them; and they were never very far from the front of my mind.

It is not so far from Nashville to Bardstown, but it certainly seemed, when I first walked in the door, that it was a long way from the cathedral that was my home church to the little parish gathered that day in that little building.

One of the first things that I noticed was that our choir at home outnumbered the people in this room. The procession took only half a chorus of the opening hymn rather than the customary three or four verses. I noticed, after two bars, that the piano player was not nearly as fine a musician as is our own classically trained organist, the one we somehow convinced to leave the National Cathedral in Washington to come and play for us in Nashville.

I also could not help noticing that the people in the room who turned to look and see who the newcomers were, hopeful that we had moved into the town and were about to join the parish, had already begun to measure us for spots in the choir and on the vestry and maybe among the Sunday school teachers. I could describe more things that were different, of course, the same way that you could if you were thinking about nearly any place that you have ever worshiped that is not the place with which you are the most familiar.

Then an extraordinary thing happened. Or more accurately, an ordinary thing took place that struck me in an extraordinary way. "To You all hearts are open and from You no secrets are hid," said the priest—not surprisingly, since that is what is printed in the prayer book. But these words surprised me into realizing that I could be anywhere on earth at that moment and walk in the door to some gathering of Anglicans and be one of them, instantly and completely.

Such a thing is true for all of us who worship regularly among the same crowd of folks and within the same larger communities of faith. But there is more to this gift, both for me and for all of us, whether our tradition is evangelical or liturgical or somewhere in between.

— • —

From time to time, I find myself in a little town deep in the heart of the Mississippi Delta. The lady who was kind enough to marry me is from that part of the world, and she seems to like me well enough to still take me along with her when she goes to visit her family and friends there. We have been there around Christmas almost every year that we have been together, and for some years now, I have risen early on Christmas mornings to worship with the Catholic community nearby. The liturgical dance of worship is almost the same as the one at the Episcopal church we visit for the midnight Christmas Eve service. The rooms are different and the faces are different and the music is different, but by and large the liturgy is the same. Or at least it is enough the same that I am a participant and not just an observer.

The truth, I have come to discover, is that I can wander into virtually any liturgical community—Catholic, Episcopalian, Lutheran, to mention some that I visit the most frequently—on any given Sunday and be at home in a way that I never thought was possible. Not at home in the sense of knowing everyone or being known by everyone there, but in the sense of being gathered together with all of those who call themselves Christians and who would worship the One Who made us.

Over the years, I have worshiped in all manner of places and in all manner of styles. Part of that is because of the path that my own journey has taken me: from the Nazarene Church to the Methodist Church and now to the Episcopal Church. Part of it too is that I was raised in a family that published religious music, and my father's work and later my own took me all over the country and into all sorts of worshiping communities often enough that I am able to note some of the differences among us. Often enough that I am able finally to glimpse the liturgical ties that bind us as well. Often enough that I have begun to see myself in a long line that has been, and still is, marching in from Rome to Bardstown and everywhere in between.

— • —

The way that we Christians worship and much of its form and shape and content can be traced from ancient times to the present day.

Justin was a teacher in the church in second-century Rome. Having converted to Christianity at Ephesus some years before, he wrote a letter to a friend explaining his personal journey to Christianity and describing some of the practices of the faith.

The document has come to be known as The Apology of Justin the Martyr, because his journey ended when he was martyred in Rome. But the letter that he wrote and its testimony to the way the community began to gather and why, and what happened when they did has become the point of origin for Christian worship. Wherever you go and whatever your community does in the name of worship, it has its roots in the words of that ancient letter.

— • —

On Sunday we all have an assembly at the same place in the cities or the countryside, and the memoirs of the apostles and the writings of the prophets are read as long as time allows. When the reader has finished, the president makes an address, an admonition, and an exhortation about the imitation of these good things. Then we all arise together and offer prayers; and … when we have finished there is brought up bread and wine and water, and the president offers in like manner prayers and thanksgivings, as much as he is able, and the people cry out saying the Amen.

— • —

The distribution and sharing is made to each from the things over which thanks have been said, and is sent to those not present through the deacons. The well-to-do and those who are willing give according to their pleasure, each one of his own as he wishes, and what is collected is handed over to the president, and he helps widows and orphans, and those who are needy because of sickness or for any other reason, and those who are in prison and the strangers on their journeys.

— • —

Justin mentions the president as being the person in charge, a title that no doubt changed over the years into the terms that we use now for those who officiate at our collective worship. And Justin does not mention the singing of hymns and songs of praise, but we know that singing hymns was part of the pattern of worship because it is discussed at some length in other documents from the same period. By and large, however, the pattern that he describes is the same pattern we follow today.

— • —

This basic framework for the regular worship of the church has been in place now for centuries: gathering on Sunday mornings, singing hymns and songs of praise, reading from the ancient texts; hearing an address of admonition or exhortation or instruction, praying collectively, bringing forth the gifts of wine and water and bread to be shared with all after thanksgivings have been said, taking offerings of money to be used for the work of the church and for taking care of the poor, and people responding by saying Amen (So be it).

It was this basic framework that formed what is known in parts of the church as the rhythm of the mass—praise, confession, the Word, going forth. This fourfold movement of the service of worship can be found in any Sunday morning worship service, regardless of the denomination or the tradition. In any service, the work of the people is to praise and honor God, to confess both who God is and who they have been in return, to come face-to-face with the Word of God as it is read and proclaimed and broken and shared, and to go forth to be the body of Christ in this world. We may be several churches, even dozens of churches, I suppose, but we are one church.

After Constantine relieved the church from its days of persecution, there followed a great period in which the worship of the church moved from the intimate, small, and informal gatherings described by Justin to a more elaborate and public worship. That move was reflected both in the buildings themselves and in what went on inside them.

As more and more people came into the church, there was considerable concern about heresy, and there was much misunderstanding about great theological issues such as the

Trinity and the Incarnation. Fixed liturgies for worship, in terms of both form and language, were seen as a way to help protect the church as it grew.

By the middle of the fifth century, the great liturgies of the Eastern Church had largely been fixed—the liturgies of St. James, St. Mark, St. Basil, and St. Chrysostom. These liturgies, or derivatives of them, are still in use in the East today.

In the West, the process of arriving at fixed liturgies took a little longer than it did in the East. But by the time of Pope Gregory in Rome, at the end of the sixth century, the Gregorian Sacramentary was firmly set. It, along with its beautiful plainchant, became the basis for the liturgy of the modern Roman Church. Though in various other parts of the world—Spain, England, and France—various combinations of rites and liturgies were developing, these soon faded out after Charlemagne's ninth-century establishment of the Roman liturgy as the liturgy of preference throughout his dominions.

The Reformation movement in the sixteenth century brought about, of course, a widespread set of changes in liturgy and its use. Lutherans, Anglicans, Presbyterians, and others took the basic Roman rites and adapted and modified them according to their emerging traditions. The rethinking of the ancient rituals and the subsequent modifications of them continued into the twentieth-century world, as the rise of the evangelical movements took place.

The differences in liturgies and worship styles and traditions are clear to any of us who have ever worshiped in other traditions. Yet, even so, there is a clear sense of the ancient roots of the liturgy of worship as a whole. One can still see the rhythm of the mass in any Sunday morning service of Christian worship, provided that one is willing to look. And if one is, then one can see that we are brothers and sisters to one another and not really strangers at all. And that is the gift that has been given to us, and it is to be found in the history of the whole church. That is the gift to be found for those who would come to the Table.

— • —

There is, of course, a sense in which exactly what happens in our worship services is as varied as are the places themselves. What happens in the name of worship in the living room of a house church can be, and probably should be, very different from what happens in the great cathedrals.

Whenever I am in Mississippi, there is a chance that I will attend one or two of three different churches while I am there. At one of them, the service begins with a procession that moves to the music of an old hymn. At another a song leader leads us all in singing modern praise choruses after the pastor has come in and greeted us all with a hearty, "Good morning.

Praise the Lord!" At another, there is a sort of three-piece house band that does a number or two so that people know that the service is about to start and that it is time to stop talking amongst themselves.

At one of the churches, before we take the Eucharist we make no formal confession at all. At another, we say our confession together on our knees after the sermon and before the prayers of the people. At the other, we fall to our knees and confess almost before anything else is done at all, like the Lutherans that I used to visit at my grandfather's church.

At one of them, when it is time for Communion, we move in rows and kneel at the altar and drink from a common cup. At another, they pass a tray through the congregation, and we each take a little cup from the tray and drink grape juice. At the third, we stand in a kind of receiving line and move in a circle until it is our turn to dip our bit of bread into the cup that is held by the server.

It is all very different. And it is all the same.

The ancient pattern for worshiping God and celebrating the Eucharist is the basis of our common life. The faithful have been practicing this same rhythm of worship—praise, confession, the Word, going forth—since the first or second century after Christ. And in many ways, nothing that we have done to codify it or to modernize it or to adapt it to our own times and our own places and our own sense of who we are as communities of faith has changed its essential nature. It is still the same, whether we realize it or not.

This liturgy—the work of the people—has been passed down to us through centuries of devotion and practiced by those who have gone before us. It has been shaped and reshaped in ways that reflect the changing nature of our cultures and our theologies. It has been modernized often so that its language is made clearer to those who sit in the pews. It has been studiously massaged to emphasize one part of it or the other so that it more closely mirrors and leads a particular community of faith at a particular time.

But at its heart, it is the same—gather, praise, read, exhort, bring gifts, offer thanksgivings, share the meal, say our prayers, offer up resources, take care of the poor. Whether the setting is formal or casual whether the room is large or small, simple or ornate; whether its art is patterned after the ancient or after the contemporary, we hold these things in common. And we hold them in common not only with those in the room in which we gather, not only with those whose denominational label we share, not only with those whose worship style and theological posture are the same as ours, but we hold these things in common with all Christians everywhere, from time past into time present into time to come.

—•—

As we sit in our places on any given day of the Lord, we might look around at those who enter the room and take up their places as well. Some of them, maybe even most of them, are people that we know. Some of them come bearing burdens, and some of them come with joy and hope in their hearts. Some of them are lost and afraid, and some of them are confident and strong. But all of them belong to us in some way that has been shaped and refined by the act of worship that is about to take place.

One might also remember that this is not the only room where that is true. It is also true in countless thousands of other places this very morning as well. The buildings may look different and the bits of pieces of the dance may be practiced differently, but these are our brothers and sisters; and they are with us now, in this moment, in this place.

— • —

Something begins the worship, some signal that moves us from our private thoughts to our collective ones: a knock on a prayer bench resounds, and chanting begins. Or a bell rings out the Angelus. Or a minister rises from a chair in the chancel to read out a versicle to which all respond in unison. Or a musician plays the first chords of a hymn, and all rise up to sing. Or a choir enters in processional.

And when this signal is given, here on this "day that is named for the sun," as one translation of Justin's letter has put it, we who respond to the invitation to raise a song to the Lord, a shout of triumph to the Rock of our salvation, would do well to remember that we are not alone.

The ones who have gone before us, all the ones who raised up this Ebenezer and the ones who were before them and the ones who will come after us are here with us as we gather up on this day of the Lord. And brothers and sisters whose names and places we do not know are gathered with us at this very moment as well. In their places too, they wait in silence and in prayer and in reverence and in anticipation.

All of our brothers and sisters for all time are with us, in this very moment, in this very place, for this very purpose—to praise and honor God, to hear God's Word, and to feast at the Table of the Lord.

CHAPTER 4

The Word Proclaimed

FROM THE PSALTER

I will remember the works of the Lord,
and call to mind your wonders of old time.
I will meditate on all your acts
and ponder your mighty deeds.

A PRAYER FOR ILLUMINATION

Open our hearts, we pray, by the power of thy Holy Spirit,
that as Scriptures are read, and the Word proclaimed, we
may hear with joy what you say to us today. Amen.

A PRAYER FOR ILLUMINATION — FROM THE HOLY EUCHARIST

The Word of the Lord.
Thanks be to God.

There is a moment within each service of worship when someone rises and makes his or her way to the lectern to read from the Hebrew Scriptures. Some ancient passage, thousands of years old,

47

is read aloud, and we listen for its wisdom or its prophecy or its narrative of the way that God has always been with us. Then there is silence while we contemplate its meaning for us on this day and at this place in our lives.

In response, a psalm is read by someone or by all of us responsively, or chanted by a soloist and a choir. We listen to the words of the ancient prayer book of the Bible, and we listen for the prayer of God that rises in our hearts on this day, the prayer of God that can only be prayed through each of us, individually, from out of the place within us where God speaks only to us.

Another one of us rises, someone appointed to recreate the moment when somewhere in the early days of the faith, one of the deacons of the community that gathered at Ephesus or Rome or Philippi stood up and said, "We have received a letter from Paul." We hear from the words of those letters to the early church, the ones full of wonder and power and struggle, that sought to guide those who came before us as to what it meant to follow the One Who Came. And there is silence again.

The silence is broken by the offering of an Alleluia, a simple chant that is sung by us all as we stand to await the reading of the Gospel. That reading is preceded by the ceremony of the acolytes with their candles, coming down from the chancel and leading a priest holding a book. We turn and watch so that soon we are all facing one another. The procession and the Alleluia both stop as the priest reaches the center of the sanctuary and stands among us, reminding us of the coming of the Light into our midst and the presence of God Incarnate among us still. "The Holy Gospel of our Lord Jesus Christ," the priest intones. "Glory to you, Lord Christ," we reply together, and then the priest begins to read the lesson for today.

Then this one who has been given to us to be our priest and minister and leader, this one who has been called forth from among us to guide us in our journeys, will proclaim the Word. Some ministers are better at this part than others. Some of them are poets and others of them are teachers and others are storytellers and others are pastors more than preachers. But all of them have been given to us and to God and to the Story itself. And we listen and we hear and we seek the Word among their words.

— • —

Frederick Buechner, in his book *The Sacred Journey*, once wrote that "the story of any one of us is the story of us all." I have come to believe that is true over the years, years filled with both the telling of my own story and the listening to the stories of others. No story, clearly and artfully and honestly told, fails to find a way to sidle up to my own story and stand next to me, drawing me into it and into my own. It generally fails to happen only when I am not paying attention, either to others or to their words or to my own life.

"One does not put things on paper to create masterpieces," wrote Etty Hillesum in *An Interrupted Life*, "but rather to gain some clarity." My work, at least as I have come to see it and understand it, is to try to tell my own story with some degree of clarity and art.

My hope is that if I tell my story clearly enough, I will come to understand its twists and turns, and then perhaps even its meanings. At the very least, I hope to be able to recognize some of the places where the Almighty God has been present within it.

The art, if I can muster it up from time to time, is for those who are kind enough to read my work. If I can tell my story artfully enough, then perhaps those who read it will, at the end of the telling, be able to hear something of their own stories within it. In the end, the object is not so much that people will know my story so much as it is that they will know their own story a little better.

But I have also come to believe that the sentence that Mr. Buechner wrote can be read another way. I have come to believe that "the story of us all is the story of any one of us" as well. And the great Story of us all is precisely the one that is read to us in bits and pieces in our sanctuaries each and every time we gather to worship the One Who made us and Who somehow has mysteriously authored the Story as well.

— • —

We who call ourselves Christians are sometimes referred to, among other things, as People of the Book. A large part of our faith and our way of worshiping is in fact based in the reading of the ancient texts. This is no surprise, given the roots of our faith. Our Jewish ancestors in the faith were People of the Book as well.

Each time that people of the Jewish faith gather for prayer and for worship, a part of the time is given over to the reading of and discussion of and explanation of the words of the story of God's people and the words of the prophets and the wise men and women of the Hebrew tradition. Each time they gather, the scrolls are opened and a passage or two is read in the hearing of those who are assembled.

Our Christian fathers and mothers, those who met in the houses and catacombs and rooms, were Jewish Christians, of course, and they carried with them that ancient tradition. For them, the story of the Messiah, God with us, was not separate from the story of the people of Yahweh. The reading of the ancient texts was accompanied by readings from the more contemporary texts that were beginning to emerge in those first few hundred years after Christ. And those newer texts became central to the worship practices that were being formed and shaped in the early days of our tradition.

As time passed, new things were added to the body of texts that came to be read. The memoirs of the apostles, as Justin called them, began to take shape as the Gospels and the letters and other writings that we have come to know as the New Testament. Translations into Greek and Latin and other languages took place. Over the centuries there were turning points in the history of the reproduction and distribution of the Scriptures: the ancient councils that established the canon; the shift from scrolls to books; the painstaking labors of love and devotion throughout the Middle Ages that kept the ancient texts alive in manuscripts; the advent of the printing press that made widespread distribution of the Bible a possibility; the gradual shift of our societies from illiteracy to literacy; the change from Latin into the vernacular that made it possible for more and more of us to hold and read the Scriptures ourselves.

Each of those moments in history had a particular and powerful effect on the way that we live our lives as the People of the Book.

— • —

But the most marvelous part of it all to me, in a way, is what happens to the scriptures each time we gather together to worship.

"Remembering," writes Fredrica Harris Thompsett, "is one of the important ways that we live with one another and with

God: as Christians we are called to the sacred, sacramental task of remembering."

Each time we gather, we are asked to become again what our forebears were in the first place—hearers of the Story. We are asked to go from being moderns to being ancients, to go from being studiers and scholars of the Bible to simply being hearers and listeners to the Story of us all. We are asked to stop working on the Word with our pens and our study helps and our discussion questions. We are asked to set aside our theological positions and our notions of being all-wise interpreters of the ancient texts.

We are invited to stop working on the Word and let it work on us instead. There is a mystery, of course, in the way that any story can work on a person, but for it to be this Story is even more mysterious. And as it works on us, it pulls at us to come to grips with the whole story, including the part that we come to the Table to celebrate each time we gather for worship on the sabbath. And that is another mystery, of course—the Divine Mystery.

—•—

In certain parts of the church, the pattern of readings each Sunday is guided by the system known as the common lectionary. There are particular patterns and cycles to the readings from the Old Testament, the New Testament, and the Gospels that correspond to the seasons of the church year and to the high points in the Story, the holy days, and such. The lectionary has been revised more than a little bit over the years, and it is now used by a number of different denominations within the church. It seeks to bind both the Story and the worldwide community into a whole as we worship.

One of the results of this is that one can enter any of a number of different churches—Methodist, Lutheran, Anglican, or Catholic—on any given Sunday, and the readings that you hear will pick up right where last week's left off, even if you were in another kind of community the week before. Another result is that over a period of three years, if you follow the lectionary faithfully week by week, you will hear the Story told through again. You will hear the whole story and not just the parts that a particular church or denomination wants you to hear.

The best part is that you will be immersed in the Story itself. So that the possibility exists that you will begin to more clearly see your own story in the Story of us all—including the part of the Story that tells of the things that Jesus did and said around the supper table that night so long ago. We cannot separate the story of the Table from the Story itself. It is the place where the Word Made Flesh took on an astonishing and powerful new meaning, powerful enough that we come to these places two thousand years later simply to remember that Story and to reenact it as best we can. It is the place where the Story ends and the place where it begins anew at the same time.

— • —

What matters the most is not so much whether the Story is told to us using one lectionary or another, or whether the lessons are read by white-robed folks with astonishing voices, or whether chants are sung in between. These things have meaning in and of themselves only insofar as they accurately reflect and nurture the traditions of our communities, and insofar as they seek to ground us in the Story itself and provide a place and a moment when that Story, or at least a portion of it, is allowed to work on us.

What really matters is the Story, of course—not how well we know it, but how well we allow it to know us.

CHAPTER 5

The Prayers of the People

FROM THE PSALTER

Ascribe unto the Lord the honor due his Name;
Bring offerings and come into his courts.

A PRAYER FOR THE DEDICATION OF A CHURCH

All times are your seasons, Almighty God,
and all occasions invite your tender mercies.
Accept the prayers and intercessions
offered in this place on this day
and in the days to come. Amen.

FROM THE HOLY EUCHARIST

We celebrate the memorial of our redemption,
in this sacrifice of praise and thanksgiving.
Recalling his death, resurrection, and ascension,
we offer you these gifts.

It feels like an intermission sometimes, this bit of business that comes next in the service. In the service of Word and Table, as it is sometimes called, we are in between precisely those two things—the Word and the Table.

It is the place in the service where we offer our confessions, those we make silently and individually as well as those we declare collectively. Someone leads us in prayer, gathering up our petitions and intercessions through the prayers of the people. The priest says the collect and then together we offer the Our Father. "The peace of the Lord be always with you," the priest then says to us, and we turn to our neighbors and greet them and wish them God's peace as well.

At the place where we worship, this is also the time when the minister stands in the front of the chancel and reminds us of the things that are printed in the bulletin and reflect the ongoing life of the community. It is the time when the choir stands to sing an anthem, to offer up a gift of song that helps to move us from the proclaiming of the Word to the preparing of the Table, where the Word will become flesh and dwell among us again. It is the time when the ushers move among us quietly, row by row, collecting our tithes and our offerings and gathering them up in the back of the room, ready to take forward to the altar when the moment comes.

There is such a time in all services on all Sunday mornings in all churches. It varies from place to place, of course, the way that it should be, given that we do not go to church in the same place, you and I. In some churches, the announcements are made before the service, and in some churches, what the choir sings is called a special instead of an anthem. In some churches, passing the peace means polite handshakes with the one or two people on either side of you; in others, you can be a complete stranger and still get three hugs and a pat on the back.

What is going on, in a way, is that we are taking a collective breath. We have entered the courts of praise, we have offered our worship as best we can, we have heard the Word proclaimed in scripture and sermon, and what is about to come next is even more astonishing still.

A friend of mine who is a priest tells of a man he met while visiting in India, a Hindu who was not only happy to meet my friend but also eager to show that he was not altogether unfamiliar with the Christian faith. "Ah, a Christian," he said to my friend. "I know Christians. You are the people who swallow God." I think of that man's remark from time to time when I am standing in my place and waiting for the moment when the Body will be broken. And I am glad to have a chance to take a deep breath and get ready for it.

— • —

At the end of the announcements, during most of the time that it takes to listen to the anthem and then present the tithes and offerings, a priest is busy arranging the Table, as though the rest of us were not even in the room. The golden book that holds the scriptures is removed to a table, and the service book containing the words of the liturgy is brought forth. A sacristan brings a bowl for the priest to wash his hands. "I wash my hands in innocence, and go around your altar, O Lord," he whispers, repeating a prayer taken from the psalmist. Then the vessels for the bread and the wine and the water are brought, each one placed just so along the table itself. The water and wine are mixed together, symbolizing the way that our baptism has brought us into new life, not only with one another, but also with the Christ himself.

There are a lot of hand gestures and head bowing as they do this work. It is a dance of sorts, in which each little movement has some root in the ancient tradition that has been handed down to us. There is ritual at work here, powerful and symbolic and unifying. Some do this dance better than others, and some performances are more elaborate than others, but they all carry the same weight of history.

"I must make my office with great care," wrote Charles de Foucauld. "It is my daily offering of fresh flowers and roses, symbolical of fresh love offered daily for the Beloved Spouse." I think of that sentence, and of the care with which good liturgists practices their art, whenever I see the table being prepared. It makes me want to be as careful with my own offerings as I can.

These prayers that we offer here—the ones we recite from the liturgy, the ones that we make with our gifts and offerings, the ones made by the movements of the priest at the table—these prayers say much about who we are, more than we really know.

"*Lex orandi, lex credendi*," wrote Prosper of Aquitane, a fifth-century theologian: The way we pray shapes what we believe.

— • —

For much of our lives, our prayer is a solitary thing. And well it should be.

We find a time and a place in the course of our days that we give over to our practice of being in the presence of God. It is formal or not so formal; and it includes scripture, perhaps, or readings from the saints and other wise ones. It includes the petitions and intercessions that we make for those we love and those who have been given to us.

We pause in our daily rounds to offer up prayers of petition or intercession as the events of the day unfold before us. We carry on bits and pieces of conversation with God in our minds and in our hearts, almost involuntarily, silently invoking the Almighty to be with us as our journey makes its twists and turns.

We have been taught, and rightly so, that our ongoing conversation with God requires this solitary attention to prayer.

Our models are drawn from the life of the Christ himself. "Go into your closet to pray, and the One Who sees you in secret will hear you in secret," he himself reminded us. We remember the stories of his going apart to pray, leaving even his closest friends on occasion to do so. We recall his admonition to be wary of those who pray in public places, lest pride enter in.

And yet, there is another side to our prayer. It is the part of our life of prayer that recognizes that we are not really alone when we pray. The side of our prayer that links us to all who have gone before and who will come after us. The part of our prayer that joins our voices "with angels and archangels who forever sing the hymns of praise." It is the prayer that we say in unison, shoulder to shoulder, heart to heart, with the whole church.

And nowhere is that prayer more in evidence than when we gather up on the day of the Lord. And nowhere is such prayer so often unnoticed and unremarked. It slips past us in a way, and with it perhaps there slips past us a way to change the way that we live our lives.

From the opening moments of the liturgy, we are collectively at prayer. Yet these prayers that we say together have often become so familiar to us that we find ourselves sort of reciting them on autopilot. To others of us, they can seem to be dry and lifeless and remote somehow, as though they had little to do with us and our daily lives.

"If a man does not pray his liturgy with sincere devotion the fault may very well be with him rather than with the form of words he is saying," cautions Massey Shepherd. "The real question is not whether the prayers used in worship are freely composed by those who pray or are the written words of an ancient service book. The fundamental thing is whether or not the words of prayer and praise are uttered in sincerity and truth."

"To whom all hearts are open and all desires known," we pray together in anticipation of the act of our worship itself. We say the collect for the day or the season, the prayer that places us firmly at a moment in time within the whole Story of God and the People of God. In doing so we remind ourselves that we are not the only motley crew that has gathered to worship on this day.

We pray that we may hear with joy what the scriptures have to say to us today. We say Amen as the priest invokes the ancient prayer before he proclaims the Word from the pulpit: "Let the words of our mouths and the meditations of our hearts be acceptable in thy sight, O Lord, our strength and our redeemer."

"Let us pray for the church and the whole world," says the reader, who leads us in the prayers of the people, systematically and thoughtfully guiding us through a series of intercessions and petitions appropriate to this day and this place and these people and all people.

"We confess that we have sinned against you," we say together. "Our Father," we say, as we repeat the words of Christ himself and pray that the Father's blessing will come and find us somehow. "Christ, our Passover, was sacrificed for us," we sing together as we prepare to keep the feast.

We join our voices with angels and archangels. We give thanks for these Holy Mysteries and for the fact that when our remembrance of the sacrifice has been made once again, God has "graciously accepted us as living members of the Body of Christ."

This is no casually tossed off editorial we, no set of accidentally or conveniently used pronouns, it is a reminder of who we are when we worship. Or at least it is a reminder of who we are to be and who we may yet become. Our prayer is not for ourselves alone, not even for our community alone.

— • —

There are at least two notions at work here, notions so rich and wondrous to me that I have yet to get over them.

One is the notion of the liturgy of the hours, the "prayer of Christ himself that is prayed through his Body for the sanctification of the day unto the Lord," as the church describes it.

The ancient tradition of the liturgy of the hours has its roots in the prayer of the psalmist—"Seven times a day will I rise to praise your name," reads the ancient prayer of the psalmist—and the ancient Jewish communities took this to heart and made it part of their practice as a worshiping community. The early Jewish Christians maintained the practice, which later became a part of the monastic traditions of the desert fathers and mothers. This daily sequence of the hours of prayer, the daily offices, is still carried on in monastic communities.

Though our practice of daily prayer and worship has changed much—few laypeople can lay claim to praying the hours—our regular participation in the Sunday worship of the church carries with it a sense of participation in the prayer that sanctifies the passage of time. And as such, it is not just for ourselves, but for all Christians everywhere, indeed all people everywhere, that we do it at all. When we pray, we pray for those who cannot or will not pray on this day. We pray for those we know and those whose names we do not know.

The other powerful notion at work here is the observation made by Paul, that we often cannot even find the words within us to express what we are feeling in our hearts; and yet we are called to do so. It is at that place that the liturgy of the church is so rich and so powerful.

There is, of course, for all of us who would pray, a genuine sense of our carrying on a private conversation with God in words that are purely our own, in our language, at our own pace, about the things that make up our lives as individuals and as communities. This "dialogue with Christ," as Brother Roger of Taizé called it, is essentially a personal dialogue and is an essential part of our walk as Christians.

At the same time, there is a real sense that we too must be a part of the ongoing prayer of the community at large. And the ancient liturgical prayers, those that make up the liturgy of the Eucharist, ensure by their very language that we offer prayer that is somehow larger, more inclusive, wider, and deeper than just our own lives and the lives of those with whom we share a house or a job or a family or a parish. It is prayer that takes us out into the larger world, keeping us from becoming too insular and too myopic. It is prayer that connects us, whether we are ready or not, to our brothers and sisters. This prayer centers us within the ongoing life of the community and the church and the whole world.

The prayers that we make together in the liturgy are not to be offered lightly or passed through without our humble attention to them. They are no intermission at all.

— • —

In some places of worship, like the one that I attend, at this point in the service a little parade forms in the back of the church. In this line, there are the ushers with the collection plates of envelopes and cards and checks and money. There are also two people whom the ushers have chosen that day to present the vessels of wine and bread at the altar. As the parade comes down the aisle, the congregation stands to say with their presence that these are our offerings of praise and thanksgiving. The acolyte stands at the altar to receive the gifts of money from the ushers. The priest stands behind the table and accepts the bread and the wine and the money as well, holding each one up for a moment before us all.

In these days of bank drafts and stewardship programs and pledge drives, they are very often hardly even tangible to us, these gifts that we bring in thanksgiving and for the work of the community to which we belong. What we give back seems paltry at times. But there it is, gathered up in silver plates, little pieces of paper and coin, reflecting our gratitude and our thanksgiving, and our admission that we have little to offer in return for the gifts we have been given by the One Who made us and is making us still.

The vessels that carry the bread and the wine hold our gifts too. "We have brought to you in thanksgiving the fruits of your creation and our labor," we say as they are taken to the altar. Our gifts are not as much as has been given to us, but they are what we have to give. They are our oblation.

I wonder what this moment must have looked like over the years. In the early centuries, each person had to bring her own wine and his own bread. In my imagination, I can see a man and his son bringing a bushel of wheat. And a woman with a basket of bread.

A farmer offering a cow or a lamb to be slaughtered and shared with those who have nothing to eat. A man carries a bag of gold coins he gained by selling a piece of property so that the funds can be distributed to orphans and widows. Someone carries clothes to give to those who have none. A woman approaches with only a coin or two, perhaps she has given all that she has.

Our offerings on this day and all such sabbaths include other things as well—our brokenness, our joy, our hope. Our anxieties and our fears, our struggles and our sorrows, our peace and our contentment, our faith and our doubt.

Our way of bringing offerings into these courts of praise is tamer now, by virtue of the nature of our culture and the way that the coin of the realm has become the coin of our offering of praise as well. Our way is more sterile now, certainly. But it is well to remember that what we do here is offer the fruit of our labor and our time and our talents. That what we offer to God here in these moments is what God has given us to begin with. And that regardless of the terms that we use to describe it—offerings, gifts, tithes, stewardship, or whatever name we use for it—it is indeed a reflection of our own gratitude and praise at a moment in time. It is a snapshot of our hearts and minds, taken in this moment before we come to the Table.

— • —

In a fondly remembered place where I used to worship, it was at this precise moment—with the altar prepared and the Table set, with the gifts having been given and received, with all of us standing in our places, all eyes to the front and to the Table—that the minister would say these words: "This is the Table of the Lord. It is not the Table of this congregation, nor is it the Table of this denomination; it is the Table of the Lord. And it is, therefore, a Table to which everyone present is invited."

We who have come here, wherever "here" is for us, whatever this room looks like or what words have been said or what the steps of the dance or the words of the liturgy are like, we have arrived at the moment for which we have come. On this day we have offered up our songs of praise and our prayers. We have heard the Word proclaimed. We have confessed who we are and who God has been to us in return. And the only proper response to it all is gratitude and thanksgiving.

A hush falls over the room and over us who have gathered to sing our praises, offer our confessions, and be reminded again that we belong to God and we are God's own people, forgiven and reconciled and grateful. The priest raises his hands. The chief moment is upon us.

In this moment, in hundreds of places, our brothers and sisters stand. "Lift up your hearts," the priest intones, invoking the words of the liturgy that has been said for hundreds of years.

"We lift them up to the Lord," we reply together.

And there it is, the gift of our hearts, the gift that God wants the most.

CHAPTER 6

The Word Made Flesh

I will offer you the sacrifice of thanksgiving,
and call upon the Name of the Lord.

A PRAYER BEFORE RECEIVING COMMUNION

Be present, be present, O Jesus,
as you were present to your disciples,
and be known to us in the breaking of bread.
Amen.

FROM THE HOLY EUCHARIST

The gifts of God for the people of God.
Take them in remembrance that Christ died for you,
and feed on Him in your hearts with thanksgiving.

It is right and a good and joyful thing, always and everywhere to give thanks to you," says the priest, and our great thanksgiving—our Eucharist—begins. The prayer that is said, the Great Thanksgiving, places us firmly in the Story of God's people, and we wait patiently, quietly, standing in our places.

With our heads bowed for a moment, we sing together the Sanctus: "Holy, holy, holy Lord, God of power and might. . . ." We kneel as the priest continues the prayer—"On the night in which he gave himself up for us"—and then, with hands outstretched over the bread and the wine, blesses them and consecrates them at certain points in the liturgy. And we watch the priest's hands as they go through those peculiar motions of lifting up and then breaking bread, lifting up and then pouring the water and the wine.

A circle has formed along the chancel behind the priest who is celebrating the Eucharist on that day. These are the sacristans, the acolytes, the choirmaster, and those who will assist. Slowly, reverently, the celebrant moves around that circle, offering bread and then the cup to those who will serve the rest of us. You can see them smile and nod, eat their bread and drink from the cup. Their faces hold what yours does—wonder and awe and anticipation.

The ushers come to the front of the nave and begin to step back, releasing one row of people and then another to take their places in the line leading to the altar. Our turn comes, and we reverence the altar as we take our places on our knees. We hold our hands up.

"The Body of Christ," someone says, and we look up to meet his or her eyes as the bread is placed in our hands. "The Blood of Christ," says another, tilting the cup in our direction so we can drink from it. Round and round the circle go those who serve. Round and round in another circle go those of us in the nave.

We return to our seats, and by then there is music. An anthem is sung by the choir, sometimes two. We sing a hymn together, we who are seated now, the ones who have eaten and the ones who are awaiting their turn at the Table of the Lord.

We watch as the others go to the front, our friends and our fellow parishioners. Sometimes we see friends we have not seen in a while, and we see people that we do not know by name but only by sight. We watch as people bring their young children and smile as the children come to the Table as children always do— fidgety, sometimes loud, with big eyes and grins and open hands. Others take their infants, too young for the cup and the bread, and hold them up for a blessing. We watch as a priest and an assistant come down from the chancel to serve those who cannot move to the altar to partake.

I am reminded of other times I have been in this room and have taken this meal with these people. There was the day that my heart had been broken only a day or two before by the sudden death of a loved one. And the day that we had news at our house that caused us such joy that we could hardly stand it. I remember sometimes the first day that I stood here for this purpose with these people. And I remember other times and other places as well, the weddings and the funerals and the retreats and the vigils.

I remember some of the other names for this act and am reminded of their meanings: "Holy Communion," the name that reminds us that it is through this sacrament that we enter into communion with God and with one another in order to unite our purposes with the kingdom of God. "The Great Sacrifice," recalling to us that this is indeed a commemoration of the sacrifice made for us upon the cross, calling us again to self-sacrificial love for one another. "The Holy Eucharist," the name that bears witness to our sense of thanksgiving for the good things given to us by Christ's life, death, and resurrection. "The Lord's Supper," reminding us that we are indeed nourished by this act and by the Christ who freshens and strengthens us with his presence. Whatever names we have used, in whatever kinds of places we have been, we have kept this feast before, we have made this offering of praise and thanksgiving before, and we are glad to do it again.

And sometimes this act reminds me of one of our friends and of a night when at her table we celebrated a similar meal that taught me much about this meal that I take each Sunday.

— • —

Our friend is involved in the same business that we are, and she knows a fair amount about the relationship between our work and our religion. Our common interests have made it possible for us to begin to carry on a kind of running conversation about the nature and role of religion in our lives, even though we are of different faiths: We are Christians, and she is Jewish.

We both have an interest in and a curiosity about the rituals and the practices of faithful people. We talk a lot about such things together from time to time. She has come to the cathedral with us a time or two for services on holy days, and she has even come to our house for Christmas Eve dinner and for a party that we give on Twelfth Night.

In the past two years, she has been kind enough to invite us to her house at Passover for the Seder, the ritual meal held in Jewish homes in honor of the holy day. On the first of those occasions, I learned something about the Eucharist that I think I was supposed to already know, having been raised in the church and having spent my life in and around it and in the company of the faithful. I am almost certain that I knew this thing in my head, but it had somehow never really quite worked its way into my sense of the practice and the ritual of my own faith.

This is what I learned about the Eucharist while sitting at a table with a dozen or so people on a Passover evening: Before the ritual meal that we take together on Sunday mornings took on its Christian nature and shape and form, it was a ritual meal in the Jewish tradition. Perhaps it was even the Passover meal—at least that is what scripture tells us—the Jewish ritual meal that celebrates the delivery of the People of God.

I think of that friend's house and her table often when I am in the Lord's house and at his Table. And that is because her table and his Table were once the very same in a way that has come to hold deep meaning for me.

Sitting around my friend's table that first time at the Seder, I listened and even participated as the book with the Story was passed around the table from person to person. Such a meal is a long, complicated affair with many dishes and rituals and customs as to what is eaten when and what is read before and after each dish. One of us would read from the story of God and his people and the ways that the story of those people went back and forth through the ages. Much of it was familiar to me, of course, this old story that we hear and have heard over and over again in the Old Testament. Then there would be a prayer or a declaration or a blessing, and we would eat a part of the meal as we sat around the table together, telling stories and laughing. And in this case, because we had not been to a Seder before, we had lots of questions that the others answered, about the different parts of the ritual and the way it has been practiced over the years.

I was moved by the whole evening—by being invited to participate in such holy day festivities in the first place, and then by the story of God's covenant with his people and by the way that it was read and told. I found myself wishing that we had such a ritual in our tradition. And then on the way home, I remembered that we do.

— • —

The last supper did not occur in a vacuum; Jesus did not create the prayers said during that meal out of nothing. The act of blessing God for gifts of mercy and deliverance had a particular ritual shape in Judaism. Blessings, or *berakoth*, were made according to traditional patterns of blessing God for saving actions in the past and pleading for that same saving action now. Beyond the words of blessing, the meal itself unfolded according to a definite ritual pattern. Bread and wine were blessed at prescribed moments, and only certain persons

could be present for the final solemn prayer. The
supposed informality and spontaneity of Jesus' final
meal with his disciples was not so simple or so new.

So writes Jeffrey Lee in *Opening the Prayer Book*, reminding
us that these are the roots of the ritual of the shared meal
that some of us call the Eucharist.

— • —

In those early days of our faith, the Christians were primarily
Jewish. It is true that Jesus directed his disciples to go and preach
to the Gentiles, and it is true that they did. But in the beginning
and for decades after he had gone from among them, the faith was
nurtured and developed and passed on among those who had
been Jews first and Christians second. Their practices and customs
and traditions and rituals grew out of their Jewish tradition and
history. They saw the story of Christ as the next part of the story
that they had been told and were retelling to others. It was part of
the same fabric of the story of God's relationship with us here on
earth. It was not some new story that had suddenly burst forth
out of thin air.

The patterns of their worship had its roots in the
ancient traditions of the Hebrew people. Their lifestyle and

their culture and their values were shaped by that tradition. Their sense of both their separation from the world and their inclusion in the world was shaped by that same tradition.

Much of that shaping changed over the years as Christians moved from worshiping in secret to including Gentiles into the faith and then to seeing this new faith, Christianity, become the state religion of the Roman Empire. And as the centuries have layered onto one another, the practice of the meal, the ritual of it and the custom of it and the means of it, have changed over and over again. But the practice has always had its roots in that ancient meal, a fact that many of us often fail to recognize as we gather in our houses of worship.

In the early days of Christianity, the Eucharist was in fact a meal, complete from one end to the other. It was a sort of grand potluck dinner—a way for the community to gather and break bread and share the news and check up on folks. It was a way to ensure that those who did not have enough to eat got a good meal and then went away with food that was left over from those who had more to give. These parts of the ritual meal have been pared down over the centuries. It makes our service of Word and Table no less rich and powerful, but it behooves us to remember its roots as we take our places along the altar rail.

— • —

The ritual changed over the years, as have many things about the way that we gather and worship. The meal went from dinner to ritual as time went by. The words that were said over each of the movements of the ritual changed from the telling of the whole story to telling only the high points, as it were. It takes barely a few minutes anymore for us to say and hear the words of the ancient liturgies that have moved their way across the centuries and into our varying traditions and practices. For better or for something else, these things are true.

All manner of things have come and gone or changed. Liturgies and gestures have shifted and changed. Order and form and rules about who can partake and who cannot have changed with society and culture and tradition.

There are all manner of arguments and positions about all manner of things that go on at the Eucharist. Different traditions each have their own positions about various parts of the ritual itself. There are great questions that theologians wrestle with about whether Christ is really present or whether this is all just symbolism somehow. There are questions about who can serve and who cannot, about whether gender or ordination or particular blessings have a role in choosing who can serve and who cannot. There are discussions about which sort of bread, divided in which sort of way, is proper and right. There are learned folks who wrestle with how much wine and how much water there should be and with how much of this and how much of that should be a part of the practice itself. Scholarship and discourse and argument and strife have broken out in many places over the years about just such issues. The best that can be said about such conflicts is that they are a sign that the things that make up this meal are really important to us. As well they should be.

But what really matters is this: When we gather to celebrate this meal, when we gather to "keep the feast," as the old prayer book says, however we keep the feast, we recognize that we gather in some way with those who were in the room with Christ at that first Eucharist, the night when he made that astonishing announcement, "This is my body. This is my blood."

— • —

Within each celebration of the Eucharist a pattern is at work. It is called the fourfold pattern of the Eucharist, and it has its roots in the things that Jesus said and did himself at that supper so long ago.

We are told that he took the bread, and when he had given thanks for it, he broke it and shared it among those who were gathered with him. Then he took the cup and blessed it as well and then passed it around to be shared among them.

Our reenactment of those four movements—taken, blessed, broken, shared—however formal or informal it may be in the place where we worship, is at the core of the celebration itself. And these things should be at the forefront of our hearts and minds as we participate in it.

As the Great Thanksgiving is offered, we must be thankful for the ways that God has been with us, collectively and individually. We must listen with care to the story of the night in which he gave himself up for us, the Story that has changed everything for us and for all time. We must reverently watch the breaking of the bread and the pouring and lifting of the cup as it is shared among us. And we must remember that we too are to be broken and shared for others.

This is the moment when all of the corners of our faith collide—scripture, tradition, reason, and experience—and are bound together by the mysterious presence of God. This is the moment in which our worship—its praise, its place, its Word, its sending forth—is at its fullest and richest and deepest. This is the mysterious moment of the Divine Mystery itself, a mystery we cannot hope to fathom or respond to without somehow having taken the steps to prepare our hearts and minds before we arrive at the Table.

— • —

"When the supper was over, he took the cup," says the liturgy. And we hear it now almost without thinking sometimes. Without remembering that it was in this moment that Jesus forever changed the covenant between God and us whom God has created. Often without thinking about how astonishing were the words that he said to his disciples at the end of the story that they had heard and told and relived through this ritual meal all of their lives. Without stopping to recall that we who have come along these two millennia later are still gathering together because of the astonishing things that those people heard the Christ say to them that night.

"This is my Body and this is my Blood," he said to them, and these words are repeated each time we gather and take the Eucharist, no matter how we gather or where we gather or what form and rituals we use when we gather.

"Do this in remembrance of me," he said to his friends, and now he says these words to us each time we gather to keep the feast. Not just to think about him, but to remember him. "To remember him is to make him present in our very midst. To remember him means to be united to him, by sharing in his self-offering," writes Massey Shepherd.

In this holy Eucharist, we are called upon to remember the Story of God with us. We are called upon to remember that everything changed after that night. We are called upon to remember him as we take the Body and the Blood and put it into our own bodies and mingle it with our own blood. We are called upon to remember that to do so, to participate in this pouring out of his Blood and the giving of his Body in this mysterious sacramental act is a call for us to be broken and poured out as well.

CHAPTER 7

The Postlude

FROM THE PSALTER

May these words of mine please my God;
I will rejoice in the Lord.†

A PRAYER AFTER WORSHIP

Grant that the words we have heard this day
be so grafted inwardly in our hearts
that they may bring forth the fruit of good living,
to the honor and praise of your holy Name.
Amen.

FROM THE HOLY EUCHARIST

Send us now into the world in peace,
and grant us grace and courage to love and serve you,
with gladness and singleness of heart.

Suddenly, quietly, it seems the Communion is over.

The ushers are always the last in line, and from our spot in the first or second pew we know that when we see them out of the corner of our eye, then it is almost done. They take their turns at the bread and the cup. Then they stand, and two of them wrestle the cushion from out of the center between the altar rails in our church, so that those who are about to leave the chancel will not have to jump over it. The housekeeping has begun.

As the hymn is finished or the choirmaster plays a variation of it—"A little walking music, maestro," I always want to say, as reverently as possible, of course—the priests and the servers go back and forth, carrying vessels to the sacristy, putting back the things on the Table that had been taken away for us to be able to have room for this meal. We sit in the pews and watch.

Then together we offer a prayer of thanksgiving for these Holy Mysteries and for having been included in the Body of Christ. We ask for courage and strength and grace to be the body of Christ in the world, in our world. A blessing is said over us, and a hymn is sung as the choir and those who were in the chancel go back up the center aisle. There is a shout in the back of the room, or as close to a shout as an Episcopalian can muster: "Let us go forth in the name of Christ!"

"Thanks be to God," we shout back, sort of. Shouting is at least one of the places where our community differs from some others I have known. But it should be a shout, knowing what I know about what is to come next.

— • —

Many days, I must confess, I am anxious to get out the door after church. I am ready to get to the ballpark for a day game, or I am hungry and I want to get to lunch, or I am tired from the week and I want to get home and have my Sunday afternoon nap. I want to spend a couple of hours with the *New York Times*, and I want to have a walk in the neighborhood and supper with my wife and children while the sun is going down and the breeze is still nice enough for sitting on the porch. Sundays are days of rest, and all of those things qualify. We all have things that we want to be about when Sunday afternoons come around.

But sometimes I hate to see the service end because it is so beautiful, this meal that we take together. I may have come into the church so tired and hungry and worn out from something or other that has happened in my life that I just want the service to go on and on forever so that I will not have to go back out there.

Sometimes I hate to see it end because I have a feeling that I just made a promise that I am not sure that I can keep. I have just promised, as I took the Body and Blood of Christ, to actually go and be the Body and Blood of Christ. And I am not always sure exactly what that means. Even the glimpses of what it means that are given to me from time to time, those things seen as through a glass darkly, one might say, are not always easy to understand or to turn into practical and everyday things.

But this is what I am called to do somehow: to take the ancient rhythm of this offering of worship—this praise and confession, this receiving of the Word and the Word Made Flesh, this being sent forth into the world—and somehow turn it into the underlying rhythm of my very own life, in my very own place, among those whom I am given to call my very own.

I am called again and again by this act of worship and thanksgiving to come to attention each day, in worship and in thanksgiving. I am to be listening fiercely for the Voice of the One Who made us, looking intently for the Presence of the One Who came among us, and seeking patiently for the One Who strengthens us. It is up to me to set time aside in my life to come to grips with the Word, to seek my own story among the Story of us all. It is up to me as well to seek the Word Made Flesh each day, to find the Christ Who walks among us even now in the faces and lives and stories that I encounter on my daily rounds. And to welcome him as my very own brother and my very own sister in the poor and in the needy, in the friend and in the stranger, in the one who is like me and in the one who is not.

I am also called to offer my prayer and intercessions each day in the communion of all who have gone before me and who will come after me, adding my prayer to the prayer that the Christ prays through his Body in the world. It is given to me to seek out and to cherish and to nurture the things that bind us to one another, even as I recognize the things that make us different from one another. It is given to me to be a living member of the whole Body of Christ, not just those with whom I am most comfortable, and to learn to live in love with those whose worship differs from mine rather than in fear of them.

I am called to offer all that I am—my time and my talent, my work and my worship, my resources and my rituals—offer it all up to be broken and shared and given away and counted as but loss for the sake of the Christ. It is incumbent upon me to be about the task of laying down my life, hour by hour, day by day, for the sake of Christ and those whom he loves, which is all of us, of course, even those that I cannot name and may never meet.

Somehow it is up to me to take all of those fine and lofty phrases and turn them into a reasonable and lively sacrifice, a sacrifice offered daily for the sake of the Christ. It is up to me to take the mystery of the Body and Blood that we have been so near at this Table on this day and turn it into something no less mysterious: the living Body of Christ in my own ordinary life.

"How we spend our days is how we spend our lives," wrote Annie Dillard in *The Writing Life*. "What we do with this hour and with that one is what we are doing." And it is just that simple and just that mysterious and just that profound, I think.

I sometimes do not want to leave the sanctuary on Sunday because I know that what must happen next, if I am to keep my promises made in this service of Holy Communion, is that I must put my hours and days and money and work and love and choices and everything else into the hands of Christ. I must do so each day, putting them there to be taken and blessed and broken and shared, no matter the cost. And I know, even as I stand in this room with my friends and fellow worshipers, filled with the joy and hope and beauty of this offering that we have made together, that such a thing requires a more perfect love than I am capable of on my own.

— • —

We have come here this day and we have entered these courts with praise. We have joined the mothers and fathers of our faith, our brothers and sisters from all across time, in saying the ancient words of prayer and worship and honor and praise.

We have sung our hymns and made our confessions. We have heard the Word read and proclaimed, we have said our prayers together, offering up our petitions and intercessions for ourselves and for those we know and for those we will never see. We have brought our gifts and our offerings, and we have partaken solemnly of the gift that has been offered us.

But that is not the end of it, not really. We cannot simply go back to our lives. "We cannot come to this feast and not be changed," said a priest once to a friend of mine. And I hope and pray that it is true.

— • —

There is an old prayer, one that we used to say from time to time in one of the communities that I worshiped in when I was younger. "We are not worthy so much as to gather up the crumbs from under thy table," it reads. There was always a sort of collective lowering of the decibel level throughout the congregation when we said this. None of us really wanted to acknowledge "our manifold sins and wickedness." This was back in the days of *I'm Okay, You're Okay*. We were, most of us, fairly sure that we were unworthy for a lot of reasons, but it seemed better not to say that too loudly.

There is another old prayer that we say from time to time in the liturgy in the church that I now attend. "Forgive us when we come to your table for solace alone," it says. It is a reminder that the things we have done here are not the end at all. First and foremost, we are to worship God. Second, and whatever the next word is, second most, I suppose, we are to be the Christ in this world to our brothers and our sisters.

"The journey we make into ourselves," wrote Elizabeth O'Connor about another part of the journey of faith, "is not in order that we think poorly of ourselves, be made humble and dependent, but in order that we touch our divinity—know firsthand that superior essence that dwells in us. You and I are called to vast things . . . full inside for our own sake, and for the sake of each other, and for God's sake."

— • —

I like the feeling of never wanting to see the service of Word and Table come to an end. It is so pretty and so fine and so powerful and so rich, most days I just want to stay forever.

"And there are countless hosts of men and women and children in every generation and in every coast and clime who go to worship in order to see him lifted up in word and sacrament, and in the visible charity of his Body, the Church. The more clearly they see him there, the more dearly they love him there," writes Massey Shepherd. I have to confess that I dearly want to be in that number whenever they go marching in. And if they decide to linger in the building awhile and sing one more hymn, most days I will be happy to stay with them.

But Shepherd speaks of more. "And in that love their lives are conformed more and more to his image and likeness.

Worship becomes, therefore, both the means and the end of attaining our lives' fullest powers and possibilities—where we are 'made one body with him, that he may dwell in us, and we in him.'" I want to be in that number too.

— • —

Depending on which way we turn down the street on Sundays, when we pull out of the parking lot and head to lunch, I can see at least two of the steeples, sometimes all three, that rise above the three places where I have learned about what it means to share in the gifts of God for the People of God.

And on my way home through the neighborhood, I will pass more such places, places that I have never attended and never will, most likely, save the odd wedding or funeral. There are many places like that where you live, too. Some of them are places where the way that worship is done would be a strange thing for me to participate in, places where the building itself and the liturgy and the customs are very different from what I am used to. There are other places where I would feel right at home.

What I try to remember when I drive by these places is that within them and without them now, on this day of all days, there are hundreds and thousands who will enter such doors with thanksgiving and make their offerings and hear the Word and break the bread and drink the cup. And then we will go forth to try to be Christ to one another and to those who are given to us, in our neighborhoods and our schools and our jobs, and wherever else it is that we go.

And that is the reason that we go into such places at all. That is the reasonable and lively sacrifice that God wants from us. That is what it means for us to pray that we may worthily receive the Lord. That is what the liturgist meant when he wrote the prayer that begins our worship, the prayer that we say in the hope that we too may perfectly love Him.

No one makes a spiritual journey alone, no matter how solitary such a journey seems at times. We are surrounded by a great cloud of witnesses. Sometimes among the clouds, so to speak, it is possible to identify some of those witnesses who have walked beside us for a certain part of our journey, and to whom we owe many thanks.

The authors whose names appear below (along with the titles of specific works they have written that mean much to me in my own experience of the mystery of the Eucharist) have been fine companions to me in this part of my journey, and I am grateful to them and for them. Some of them are quoted in this work, some are not—all of them are highly recommended.

Bernardin, J.B. *An Introduction to the Episcopal Church* (Harrisburg, PA: Morehouse Publishing, 1983).

Broderick, Robert C., editor. *The Catholic Encyclopedia* (Nashville, TN: Thomas Nelson, 1988).

Buechner, Frederick. *The Sacred Journey* (New York: Harper & Row, 1982).

Dillard, Annie. *The Writing Life* (New York: Harper & Row, 1989).

Foucauld, Charles de. *Meditations of a Hermit* (Maryknoll, NY: Orbis Books, 1999).

Harris Thompsett, Frederica. *Living With History* (Harrisburg, PA: Cowley, 1999).

Hillesum, Etty. *An Interrupted Life: The Diaries of Etty Hillesum, 1941–1943* (New York: Pantheon Books, 1963).

Klein, Patricia. *Worship Without Words* (Orleans, MA: Paraclete Press, 2000).

Lee, Jeffrey. *Opening the Prayer Book* (Harrisburg, PA: Cowley, 1999).

Livingstone, E.A. *The Oxford Concise Dictionary of the Christian Church* (Oxford, England: Oxford University Press, 2000).

Lyman, Rebecca. *Early Christian Traditions* (Harrisburg, PA: Cowley Publications, 1999).

O'Connor, Elizabeth. *The Eighth Day of Creation* (Waco, TX: Word Books, 1979).

Price, Charles and Louis Weil. *Liturgy for Living* (New York: Seabury, 1979).

Saliers, Don. *The Soul in Paraphrase* (New York: The Seabury Press, 1979).

Shepherd, Massey. *The Worship of the Church* (New York: Seabury, 1952).

Underhill, Evelyn. *Worship* (London: Nisbet & Company, 1936).

I am also grateful to the people of Paraclete Press who first published this book—to Lillian Miao for saying yes to the notion of it; to the others there that I do not know by name but who treated my work with respect and kindness; and especially to Lil Copan, first and most decorated member of the Order of the Red Pencil (may her tribe increase).

And to Robin Pippin and my other friends at Upper Room Books for giving this little book a new life.

Finally, I am grateful to Miss Jones of Merigold, without whose help I would make no books at all.

*H*ere is a simple plan for a one-hour, weekly group discussion based on *That We May Perfectly Love Thee*. It is suitable for church school classes, book groups, retreats, or other such gatherings. One person may act as convener, or the role can rotate among group members. You may choose to light a white Christ candle each week to signal the beginning of your time together.

OPENING

Convener: Let us come into the presence of God.
Others: Lord Jesus Christ, thank you for being with us. May we hear your word to us as we speak with one another.

DISCUSSION

Convener asks others to share their impressions of the chapter assigned for the week. Use the questions and comments found on the following pages as a guide to this time of discussion.

PRAYING TOGETHER

Convener says: Based on today's discussion, what people and situations do you want us to pray for now and in the coming week? Convener or other volunteer then prays about the concerns named.

DEPARTING

Convener says: Let us go in peace to serve God and our neighbors in all that we do.

Adapted from The Upper Room *daily devotional guide, January-February 2001.* © *2000 The Upper Room. Used by permission.*

CHAPTER 1: THE VOLUNTARY

Robert Benson claims that, as a mystery, Holy Communion should be approached with reverence and awe.

- What is your earliest memory of Communion? How often was it observed? How were the elements served? Did you kneel or stand? How did the method receiving the sacrament affect you?

- In what ways (if any) do you prepare yourself for receiving Holy Communion?

- In what ways does your earliest memory of Communion affect how you now prepare for and receive the elements?

- What one word would you choose to describe Communion? Why?

- The Voluntary may have originally been a musical piece that the church organists improvised as an personal offering. In what ways does the sense of freedom reflect your experience of Holy Communion?

CHAPTER 2: THE ENTRANCE

Robert Benson describes how his personal journey from one tradition to a second to a third has shaped how he views and experiences Holy Communion.

• Recall the story of how your faith community began—or find out about it. How do current worshipers carry forward the practices on which the church was started?

• Recall places where you have worshiped. How have different settings affected the way you worship?

• Where and when have you most sensed the worldwide communion of Christians?

CHAPTER 3: THE WORK OF GOD

Robert Benson observes that one benefit of learning the history of the order of worship is that "one can see that we are brothers and sisters to one another, and not really strangers at all."

• In what ways does your participation in worship and the sharing of the elements unite you with all believers, not only past and present but also across all denominations?

• How would you describe this "gift" in your own words?

• What effect does this knowledge about the order of worship have on you?

CHAPTER 4: THE WORD PROCLAIMED

In this chapter, Robert Benson writes about the central place that scripture holds in our orders of worship.

- Recall a time when a passage of scripture has spoken to you powerfully. Reflect on that experience: Where were you? How did you feel? In what ways has that experience shaped the way you live your life?

- The author quotes Frederick Buechner's comment that "the story of any one of us is the story of all of us." How does Robert Benson's story remind you of your experience of worship and the sacrament of Communion in particular?

- Name some times or moments in your faith story when you particularly sensed God's presence.

CHAPTER 5: THE PRAYERS OF THE PEOPLE

Robert Benson describes the part of the service when we transition from hearing the Word proclaimed to receiving the Holy Mystery as a time when we, as a congregation, take "a collective breath."

• Prayers are an important part of the transition from hearing the Word to receiving sacrament. What different types of prayers does your worship community incorporate? How does each of these types help prepare you for what is to come?

• Which type of prayer is the most meaningful to you? Why?

• Without worrying about which sequence is "right" or "proper," what are the implications of offering your gifts before receiving the sacrament? What are the implications of offering them after the sacrament?

CHAPTER 6: THE WORD MADE FLESH

Robert Benson calls the early Christian practice of the Eucharist a "sort of grand potluck dinner."

- How does knowing the history of the liturgy affect your understanding of Holy Communion today?

- What do you take away from Robert's story about attending the Seder feast?

- If Holy Communion calls you to be "broken and poured out as well," what might that look like in your life and in your community?

CHAPTER 7: THE POSTLUDE

Robert Benson writes that at times he hates to see the service end.

• When has this happened to you? What was different about that service?

• How do you usually feel following a service of Communion?

• Think of a time when a worship service especially moved you. What made it special? Was it something in the service itself or something in your personal life?

THE PEOPLE GATHER IN THE LORD'S NAME

PROCLAIM AND RESPOND TO THE WORD OF GOD
The proclamation and response may include readings, song, talk, dance, instrumental music, other art forms, silence. A reading from the Gospel is always included.

PRAY FOR THE WORLD AND THE CHURCH

EXCHANGE THE PEACE
Either here or elsewhere in the service, all greet one another in the name of the Lord.

PREPARE THE TABLE
Some of those present prepare the table; the bread, the cup of wine, and other offerings, are placed upon it.

MAKE EUCHARIST
The Great Thanksgiving is said in the name of the gathering, using one of the eucharistic prayers provided.

The people respond—Amen !

BREAK THE BREAD

SHARE THE GIFTS OF GOD
The Body and Blood of the Lord are shared in a reverent manner; after all have received, any of the Sacrament that remains is then consumed.

Robert Benson writes and talks about living a more contemplative and prayerful life in the modern world.

He has written more than a dozen books about the search for and the discovery of the Holy in the midst of our everyday lives. His work ranges from books on prayer and spirituality to travel and gardening to baseball and the Rule of St. Benedict. They include *Between the Dreaming and the Coming True*, *Living Prayer*, *In Constant Prayer* and his most recent work, *The Echo Within*. His work has been critically acclaimed in publications as diverse as *The New York Times* and *Publishers' Weekly* and *American Benedictine Review* and dozens more.

Robert is a lifelong churchman, an alumnus of The Academy for Spiritual Formation, a member of The Friends of Silence & of the Poor, and was recently named a Living Spiritual Teacher by Spirituality & Practice.com.

Robert lives and writes and pays attention in Nashville, Tennessee. More information is available at robertbensonwriter.com. And you can follow his blog at thelongpew.com.